HOW MANY 3-CENT STAMPS IN A DOZEN?*

or
**How Logical
Are You?**

BY HERMAN HOVER

*There are twelve.
(Most people will
answer 4.)

PRICE/STERN/SLOAN
Publishers, Inc., Los Angeles

1986

14th PRINTING — JULY 1986

Copyright © 1976 by Price/Stern/Sloan Publishers, Inc.
Published by Price/Stern/Sloan Publishers, Inc.
410 North La Cienega Boulevard, Los Angeles, California 90048

ISBN: 0-8431-0408-2

Brain teasers are as old as mankind. An ancient classic is the Riddle of the Sphinx, the fabled creature with the head of a woman, body of a lion and wings. This mythological monster killed all passersby who could not answer her riddle: "What is it that goes on all fours, then on twos and finally on threes?" Oedipus, King of Thebes, came up with the answer, and the Sphinx — in a fit of frustration — destroyed itself.

Our puzzles are not as fatal; they're fun and, we hope, the kind you enjoy doing over again.

By the way, the King of Thebes' answer was *Man* — he goes on all fours as an infant, on two legs as an adult, and on three when he walks with the aid of a cane in old age.

You're the pilot of an airplane that ✈ travels from New York to Chicago — a distance of 800 miles. The plane goes 200 miles an hour, and it makes one stop for 30 minutes. What is the pilot's name?

Whatever your name is.

Can you arrange for Jane to stand ✈ behind Lee and Lee to stand behind Jane at the same time?

Yes, back to back.

Is it legal for a man to marry his widow's sister?

Legality has nothing to do with it. Only dead men have widows.

There are 10 black stockings and 10 white stockings in a drawer. If you reach into the drawer in the dark, what is the least number of stockings you must take out before you are sure of a pair that matches?

Three. You might have a pair after taking out two, but the third one must match either the black or the white stocking already removed.

A kangaroo is at the bottom of a 30-foot well. Each day he jumps up three feet and slips back two. At that rate, when will he reach the top?

On the 28th day. At the end of the 27th day, he had ascended 27 feet. On the 28th day, he reaches the top.

A rope ladder is hanging over the side of a ship. The ladder is 12 feet long, and the rungs are one foot apart. The lowest rung is resting on the top of the ocean. The tide rises four inches an hour. How long would it take before the first four rungs of the ladder are underwater?

A man and his two sons must cross a stream. The man weighs 200 pounds and his sons each weigh 100 pounds. There is a boat that can carry only 200 pounds. How will they cross?

The two sons go first; one son comes back and dad rows over by himself; the other son returns to pick up his brother.

Which would you rather have — a trunk full of nickels or half a trunk full of dimes?

The half trunk-full, since dimes are smaller and are worth twice as much as nickels.

A young boy comes home from school. He lives in a high-rise building. Some days, he gets off the elevator at the eighth floor and walks up four flights, to his family's apartment on the twelfth floor. On other days he goes right up to the twelfth floor.

Why the difference?

He's not tall enough to reach past the eighth button. So unless someone else is on the elevator with him, he must get off at eight.

A child playing on the beach had 6-1/6 sandpiles in one place and 3-1/3 in another. If he put them all together, how many sandpiles would he have?

One.

Leather shoes are worn in bowling ×
and rubber soled sneakers in tennis.
In what sport are all metal shoes
worn?

Horse racing.

A pound of gold weighs more than a pound of feathers. Right or wrong?

The feathers weigh more. Feathers are weighed by avoirdupois, according to which a pound is equal to 7,000 grains, while gold is weighed by the troy system, according to which a pound is 5,760 grains. (But once we're on the metric system, there won't be any difference.)

It takes 4½ hours for a jet plane to fly coast to coast. One plane leaves Los Angeles for New York at 4:40 o'clock, while another plane leaves New York for Los Angeles at 6 o'clock. Which plane will be closer to New York when they pass each other?

At the instant they pass each other, both will be the same distance from New York.

A country squire living on his farm
is served two freshly laid eggs for
breakfast every morning. He does
not own any hens; he does not buy,
beg or steal the eggs; he does not
trade for them or find them, and he
is not presented with them. Where
do the eggs come from?

Ducks.

On a college exam, a student was asked the following question: "Using a sextant, how would you determine the height of a building?" The student's matter-of-fact answer was: "Lower the sextant with a string and measure the string."

In the Hope family there are seven sisters, and each sister has one brother. Including Mr. and Mrs. Hope, how many in the family?

Ten — both parents, the seven daughters and just one brother.

If the Vice President of the United
States should die, who would be
President?

The President.

How many times can you subtract 2 from the numeral 21?

Only once. From then on, you would be subtracting from 19, 17 and so on.

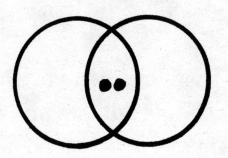

Would it be cheaper for you to take one friend to the movies twice or two friends at the same time?

Two friends at the same time. Then you would have to buy only three admissions. If you took one friend twice, you would have to buy his ticket twice and your own twice as well.

On a farm in Malaya is the world's most perfect plum tree. The main trunk has exactly 24 branches, each branch exactly 12 boughs, each bough exactly 6 twigs and each twig bears 1 fruit. How many apples on the tree?

None. Apples don't grow on plum trees.

Cleopatra was a pure blooded Egyptian queen. Yes or no?

No. She belonged to the Ptolemaic dynasty and was Greek.

When you take two apples from three apples, what do you have?

You have the two apples.

How close a relative would the sister-in-law of your father's only brother be?

Pretty close. She'd be your mother.

On an average day, what mode of
transportation carries more
passengers than any other?

Elevators.

Here is a practical joke you can play on your friends. Give them this brain teaser:

A bus starts at the depot with six passengers. It proceeds a few blocks and stops. Two passengers get off and five get on. It continues a short distance and stops. Three get off and seven board. It starts again, continues, then stops and four get off and four get on. It proceeds on its route, stops and five get on, three leave, then two more get on. On the next stop, 14 get on and no one gets off.

The puzzle sounds simple, but you will be surprised how many do not have the correct answer — because the question is: "How many stops did the bus make?" Most of your friends (if they are still your friends) will have counted the number of passengers on the bus.

How can you throw a golf ball with all your might and, without hitting a wall or other obstruction, have it stop and come right back to you?

Throw it up in the air.

Your car is facing south on a straightaway. How can you drive it 100 yards and, without making a turn, find yourself 100 yards north of where you started?

Drive it in reverse.

Standing on a hard floor, how can you drop an egg three feet without breaking it?

Hold the egg four feet above the floor. It will drop the first three feet without breaking; then catch it.

How do you pronounce V O L I X?

Volume nine.

In which book of the Bible do you read about Abel slaying Cain?

None. Cain slew Abel.

How can you put your left hand in
your right-hand pants pocket and
your right hand in your left-hand
pants pocket, both at the same
time?

Put your pants on backward.

According to the law of most states, the attempt to commit a certain crime is punishable, but committing the crime is not. What is the crime?

Suicide.

Read the following sentence once, slowly, counting the number of F's.

FINAL FILES ARE THE RESULT OF YEARS OF SCIENTIFIC STUDY WITH THE EXPERIENCE OF YEARS.

How many did you find?

If you spotted four, you're above average. And if you counted five, you can turn up your nose at almost everybody. Six is perfect.

How many cubic feet of earth are there in a hole 2 yards wide, 3 yards long and 4 yards deep?

None. There is no earth — or anything else (except air) in a hole.

If you drop a steel ball, would it ⌐
fall more rapidly through water at
20 degrees or water at 60 degrees?

Sixty degrees. Water at 20 degrees would be ice.

When somebody says, "I'll break ⌐
every bone in your body," how
many bones would he have to break
— 50, 200, 500 or 1,000?

Approximately 200.

There are 14 punctuation marks in English grammar. How many can you name? Nine is passing.

Period, question mark, comma, semi-colon, colon, quotation mark, apostrophe, dash, exclamation point, asterisk, braces, hyphen, brackets, parenthesis.

(a) What word of eight letters has seven consonants and one vowel?

(b) What word of five letters has one consonant and four vowels?

(a) STRENGTH
(b) QUEUE

What character played by Boris Karloff brought him the greatest success?

If you said Frankenstein, you're wrong. He played Frankenstein's monster. Frankenstein was the name of the scientist who created the creature in Mary Shelley's novel.

Who was Shakespeare's favorite actress?

There was none. In the Elizabethan theater, all roles were played by men and boys.

A single English word can be formed from these letters. What is it? Use all the letters:

PNLLEEEESSSSS

SLEEPLESSNESS

The amount of water flowing into a tank doubles every minute. The tank is full in an hour. When was the tank half full?

If the tank is full in 60 minutes, it was half full a minute earlier.

Two highway patrol officers concealed themselves behind a large billboard to apprehend speeders. One cop was facing up the road, the other down it so as to cover both approaches. "Mike," said one without turning his head, "what are you smiling about?" How did he know Mike was smiling?

They were facing each other.

There are two 5-gallon containers. One has 4 gallons of red fluid and the other 4 gallons of blue. One gallon of the blue is poured into the red container, and then one gallon of the now mixed 4-red to 1-blue is poured back into the blue container. Is there more red in the blue or more blue in the red container?

Exactly the same amount of red in the blue as there is blue in the red.

You've seen a map of Italy. Is the toe on the east or west side of the boot?

West side.

By what fractional part does four-fourths exceed three-fourths?

One-third.

Starting out with $32 you bet 6 times. Each time you bet one-half of what you have. Suppose you win 3 times and lose 3 times. Would you come out ahead, behind or even?

No matter which times you win or lose, you will have lost exactly $13.50.

A sophisticated computer is fed this knotty problem:

Between two clocks, one of which is broken and doesn't run at all while the other loses one second every 24 hours, which is more accurate?

The computer's answer:

The one that doesn't run at all, as it indicates the correct time twice every 24 hours, whereas the other indicates the time accurately only once every 120 years.